Rosa Parks Biography

Her Life, Struggle, and Overcoming Racism

Dillon Reed

TABLE OF CONTENTS

THE EARLY LIFE OF ROSA PARKS 1
Childhood 1
Experiencing Racism as a Young Black Girl in America 3
Rosa Parks' Educational Background 5

THE BEGINNINGS OF THE ROSA PARKS WE ALL KNOW: HER EARLY ACTIVISM 8
Meeting Raymond Parks and The Start of a Marriage 8
Rosa Parks' Associations With the NAACP 10
Involvement with the Early Civil Rights Movement 12
Rosa Parks' Experience at the Highlander Workshop 13
Emmett Till and his Influence on Rosa Parks 15

THE BUS, THE BOYCOTT, AND ALL THAT FOLLOWED 17
Rosa Parks' History with Buses 17
Taking a Stand By Refusing to Stand 20
The Arrest 21
The Boycott 23

ROSA'S LATER ACTIVISM 26
In the Years That Followed the Boycott 26
Exclusion and Being Forced to Move 28
Joining Politics 30
Rosa Parks' Health and Raymond's Death 34

THE LATER YEARS OF ROSA PARKS' LIFE, HER DEATH, AND HER LEGACY 36
   Struggling In Her Later Years 36
   The Death of Rosa Parks 38
   The Legacy of Rosa Parks 39

THE IMPORTANCE OF LEARNING THE REAL HISTORY OF ROSA PARKS 41

The Early Life of Rosa Parks

Childhood

Rosa Parks was born on February 4, 1913 in Tuskegee, Alabama. Her birth name was Rosa Louise McCauley, derived from both her maternal grandmother, Rose, and her paternal grandmother, Louisa. Born to Leona Edwards and James McCauley, Rosa's determination is said to have been gifted to her from both her parents. Leona was a teacher who attended Payne University, and her father was skilled in carpentry and stonemasonry. Both were dedicated individuals who instilled a sense of black pride in Rosa at a young age. Rosa's parents were together at her birth and shortly after, but by the time she was about a year old, Rosa's father moved north due to a lack of job security in Alabama as well as his wanderlust. Though he didn't remain in contact during Rosa's youth, her father eventually reconnected during her later years. In her biography Rosa claims her father was apologetic and remorseful of missing out on her life. After he left, Rosa was raised by a single mother with assistance from her grandparents.

The early years were difficult for Leona and Rosa. As an infant Rosa was sickly and frail. In her childhood years she struggled with recurring illnesses, specifically tonsillitis. This made child rearing more difficult for Leona during a time that was already burdensome. It wasn't until later in life that her mother was able to afford the surgery which would help Rosa live more normally without frequent illnesses. Leona struggled to find work as a teacher shortly after the birth of Sylvester, Rosa's younger brother. She was eventually hired to teach in a distant city, but this meant she would need to live there during the week. Rosa's grandparents stepped in to care for the children while Leona was away. Living with her grandparents was difficult at times. Rosa's grandparents were once enslaved. They were strict with the children and could be physically punishing at times. Rosa was known to stand up for her younger brother, as well, reminding her grandparents they were only children with no parents around.

Rosa's grandfather was born to a slave owner father and a slave mother, which caused him to have lighter skin. Despite being freed eventually, living this way taught him a great deal about how some white people treated black people, and he used his lighter skin to speak out against these mistreatments. His previous experience with white people led him to be further protective of his children and grandchildren, and he often forbade them from working in white people's homes or playing with them as children. This fear was understandable, as well, given their home was in an area that also had a high level of Ku Klux Klan (KKK) activity. Rosa's mother took time during the weekends to teach Rosa how to read early on. She tried to prepare her daughter at a young age by telling her about the world and racism in the hope she could prepare her for the years to come.

Experiencing Racism as a Young Black Girl in America

During her youth Rosa witnessed a lot of racism, especially living on the farm with her grandparents in Tuskegee. The city was known for having prevalent racism and a very active KKK circle. The local KKK group often marched through the town burning crosses and terrorizing black Americans. They burned churches and homes with no punishment from the police. Rosa often recalled sleeping in her regular clothes for fear of needing to run in the middle of the night. In addition, she recalled often falling asleep near her grandfather as he sat in a rocking chair with a shotgun in his lap. These activities only worsened after World War I. Black citizens did their best to care for one another, but ultimately each one of them needed to be hypervigilant at all times. It wasn't only these memories that taught Rosa about the racism experienced by black Americans, however. At the age of eight reading caused her to stumble upon white supremacy texts and racist theories. Her mother and grandparents encouraged both Rosa and Sylvester to have a strong sense of black pride, and Rosa's grandfather attempted to join the Pan-Africanist Universal Negro Improvement Association in support of Marcus Garvey's values and ideas. He was ultimately rejected from joining because of his lighter skin. Rosa carried black pride throughout her childhood, often questioning why things were the way they were.

Due to discovery of racist texts Rosa grew up feeling as if she would consistently need to prove herself to be anything but a beast in the eyes of most white people. It wasn't until high school that she discovered Black History as a subject and began to gain more revolutionary ways of living. She frequently witnessed the difficulties of living in a deeply segregated town. She watched as parents fought to give what little they could to better the schools for black children while the white children were given schools with heating, windows, and supplies. In addition to struggling with frequent illnesses, Rosa, like many other black children in Alabama, picked cotton as a way to bring in extra money for her family. They were paid a measly wage and often dealt with physical difficulties like hot dirt that burned their feet. If they damaged the cotton in any way, they were forced to give up their wages for the day. Even as a child, however, Rosa argued for her own well-being. Once she was scolded by her grandmother for threatening to beat a white boy with a brick, because he threatened to harm her. This was something Rosa never understood—the idea of staying quiet for safety. She refused.

Rosa Parks' Educational Background

As a teacher, Leona knew the value of a good education, and she wanted Rosa to have a much better education than the norm. After grade six there were no available educational services for black children, so Leona sought out a different form of education for Rosa. She saved what money she could and sent Rosa to Montgomery when she was 11 years old. Rosa lived with an aunt and attended Miss White's Montgomery Industrial School for Girls. After attending for half a year, Rosa was granted a scholarship in exchange for providing cleaning services to the school. While many of her classmates went off to do homework or spend time together, Rosa would spend her afternoon hours sweeping and cleaning. Rosa often discussed her education at Miss White's in a fond manner. The girls were taught skills which were necessary for jobs where black women could be hired such as sewing, cleaning, cooking, and caring for sick individuals. This was the first place Rosa learned to use a sewing machine, a skill that later gave her an opportunity to earn a living. In addition to the domestic labor skills taught, the girls at Miss White's were given lessons in English, math, geography, and other academic subjects. She was schooled by the teachers as well as the principal not to settle in her dreams or life. She was given confidence and told that her skin color wasn't going to determine her outcome in life. Despite these lessons, the school was not as progressive as it seemed. The teachers believed slavery benefited black people, because it allowed them to advance instead of living the way they had in Africa. The school never hired black educators. While Rosa and many of her classmates had a supportive experience in this school, she was forced to leave by the eighth grade, the year she was set to graduate, because the school shut down. The reasons were various: arson, aging teachers, but most importantly, a lack of support from white individuals. Miss White's teachers and staff were shunned by their communities and discouraged by the KKK from continuing to provide schooling for black girls.

Since there were no junior high schools or high schools available to black students at this time, Rosa ended up switching to a laboratory school in Alabama State College. It was there she began to truly excel in her studies. Rosa was fascinated by all she learned. She read widely and studied various subjects. Her mother had instilled a love of education in her daughter and hoped she would grow up to be a teacher, as well, but Rosa remarked that she was often discouraged by the state of the school systems. She enjoyed mentoring youth in her later years, but she never felt the school systems made it worthwhile to become a teacher. She believed it a discouraging environment. Even Miss White's school had been a harmful environment at times. Instead of education, Rosa hoped for some time to be a nurse or a social worker. She wanted to be in a career that allowed her to help ease suffering in other people or to help better their lives in some way.

While Rosa was a dedicated student, she, like many other black students, was forced to leave school because of financial and familial responsibilities. Many times throughout her life Rosa was called to care for others, including her mother, grandfather, and grandmother. While she often stated she was upset having to leave school, she knew it was her duty and did so willingly. After she left high school Rosa worked many domestic jobs including cleaning, cooking, and sewing, all while dealing with a variety of prejudices. She knew these jobs would not continue forever, and her mistreatment at the hands of white employers only propelled Rosa further into activism.

The Beginnings of the Rosa Parks We All Know: Her Early Activism

Meeting Raymond Parks and The Start of a Marriage

While attending the laboratory school or while caring for sick family members, Rosa had little to no interest in dating. Around the time she was 18 years old, a friend introduced Rosa McCauley to Raymond Parks. This was not a tale of love at first sight. In fact, Rosa had little interest in dating Raymond for a variety of reasons, including that he was lighter skinned than she. In addition, her experiences with previous romantic relationships was enough to make her not want to date men in general. However, over time Rosa grew attached to Raymond, his views, and activism. Prior to meeting Raymond, Rosa had been outspoken about her own values and unwillingness to be persecuted, but she had never met an activist. It wasn't only his views she was drawn to, however; she appreciated his boldness and willingness to fight against mistreatment even in the face of fear. Through him she learned about a variety of organizations and different ways to bring about change. She observed someone else who was willing to show his disapproval of being treated unfairly.

Rosa and Raymond married in December, 1932, but this wasn't the only major event taking place in Rosa's life at the time. The wedding occurred during a mass community effort to help the boys involved in the Scottsboro case. Raymond was actively involved with various organizations that were trying to get the boys out of jail. While Rosa would later be the one frequently away from home as an activist, in the early part of her marriage she was more often than not worried about Raymond's safety. The Scottsboro case, which involved nine boys charged with raping two white girls, was one that prompted serious conflict between police and activists. People close to the Parks were murdered in an effort to scare the remaining activists from fighting for the boys. Rosa recalled one incident in particular in which the police drove back and forth in front of her home waiting for Raymond to return. That evening Raymond was forced to sneak home and climb in through the back of the house. The Parks would frequently provide food for the boys while in jail. Raymond refused to focus on any other issue until he knew they were free. This trial ended up making history as being one that brought about change in how African Americans were treated by the Supreme

Courts. While the charges weren't completely dropped, they were able to receive shorter sentences instead of hanging and death. This was due in part to the efforts of National Association for the Advancement of Colored People (NAACP), with which Raymond Parks was deeply involved. His involvement led Rosa to join the organization, which would be one of the most life-changing decisions for her yet.

Rosa Parks' Associations With the NAACP

The NAACP began after a traumatizing lynching in 1909 that took place in Illinois and grew in strength, particularly around the time of the Scottsboro case. Originally Raymond was an active participant, but he eventually grew tired of the Montgomery chapter because of their specific values. He thought they believed themselves better than other groups because of their members being primarily middle class. Rosa had long been interested in joining the NAACP but was often discouraged by Raymond, because he believed it to be too dangerous for her to be involved. It wasn't until 1943 that she would attend her first meeting. In addition to Raymond's discouragement, she originally believed the organization was open only to men. This changed one day when she saw a newspaper photo of Johnnie Carr, a fellow classmate from Miss White's school, attending a meeting. Rosa hoped to see her old classmate, so she decided to attend, but at the December meeting only men were present. Since she was the only woman there, she was asked to write down what took place during the meeting. That meeting was also election day for the chapter. As a result of taking diligent notes, she was elected secretary. Rosa and Carr were the only two women in attendance at these meetings until Rosa's mother joined a few years later.

After the Scottsboro case, NAACP membership began to drop drastically. Rosa, Carr, and friend E.D. Nixon stayed and focused their efforts on stopping state supported lynchings and voter registration. While black Americans were beginning to be more outspoken about being mistreated, these early years in the civil rights movement were marked by bold and courageous choices by many individuals, including Rosa herself. This was a time when they were taking the risk of using the law to make changes. One such case was that of Mrs. Recy Taylor, a young mother who was gang raped by six white men. Rosa traveled over one hundred miles as a representative of the NAACP to help Taylor, who was trying to get legal assistance to charge the men with sexual assault. During these years men often assaulted black women and faced no repercussions, but many activists and writers vocalized their support of Mrs. Taylor, including notable figures like W.E.B. Dubois and Langston Hughes. While no charges were officially brought against the men, some of them changed their stories and admitted to having sex but claimed it was consensual. Mrs.

Taylor wasn't able to get justice, but the NAACP helped her relocate and find work near their chapter.

Involvement with the Early Civil Rights Movement

The early part of the civil rights movement is discussed less often, because many of the achievements were small in comparison to the later and larger wins. What people often fail to acknowledge, however, is these small victories paved the way for work that was done in later decades. Shortly after the attempt to gain justice for Mrs. Recy Taylor, Rosa focused on growing as an activist. She began attending national conferences for the NAACP, where she learned from other revolutionary women like Ella Baker. In addition, she continued working on her skills. She took a typing course taught by another woman. Baker later proved to be a close friend and inspiring mentor to Rosa, who always reminded her to focus on the younger generation with the hope of training them to take over where the elders left off. In the coming years Rosa continued attending various NAACP conferences. In 1948 she gave a strong speech demanding better treatment in the south. She lectured those who were proud should feel ashamed because of the mistreatment which occurred there, especially toward black women. The speech was inciting, and immediately following it she was elected the first ever secretary for the Alabama state conference for the National Association for the Advancement of Colored People.

Much of the work E.D. Nixon and Parks did in the late 1940s and early 1950s was advocating for a federal ban on lynchings. As part of her work, Rosa went around Alabama and nearby states documenting cases of black harassment and mistreatment at the hands of whites. She continuously worked toward recognizing and meeting with those who were sexually assaulted, who faced threats in their attempts to register as voters, and who were brutally assaulted. E.D. Nixon was president of the Alabama NAACP for some time, and Rosa was very supportive of him in this role. She was often discouraged, however, by his frequent treatment of her because of her gender. He often said she didn't have the skills to be a leader but was a diligent secretary. He appreciated her support but didn't think she was courageous. It wouldn't be until years later that he would realize and speak openly about her role in grassroots movements and her intelligence.

Rosa Parks' Experience at the Highlander Workshop

In 1955, after much convincing from her family and husband, Rosa Parks embarked on a journey to a two-week workshop at the Highlander Folk School aimed at implementing the Supreme Court decision to desegregate schools. The workshop proved to be a life-changing experience for Rosa. Originally, she was hesitant about going because of the financial toll it would take to leave work for two weeks and the cost of the bus ticket. A supporter of Rosa paid for the bus ticket, however, so that she was able to attend. The Folk School had already implemented desegregation which added to Rosa's anxieties. She was excited to see the workshop was filled with approximately half black and half white attendees but was shocked when she realized all of them would be eating, sleeping, and studying together. For many this was a completely new experience, but it was one each participant felt necessary to follow through with. In addition to the topic of desegregation, the black participants finally felt they could talk about the mistreatment they were enduring in front of white people without fear. They talked about the necessary changes which needed to take place, and they talked about the massive issues they faced daily. Being allowed to speak about their difficulties for the first time without fear of reprisal allowed for open communication regarding how to effect change.

Returning home from the Highlander workshop proved difficult in many ways. While it was a very transformative experience for Rosa, one that ultimately renewed her weakening spirit, it was one that was filled with fear. She and the other participants were set to return with a plan for immediately instilling the ruling for desegregation. This was an idea that many in Alabama and other states still highly disagreed with. It would take a lot of work, especially at the city level. Many of the people who attended the workshop were fearful of the repercussions of attending and supporting a desegregated school system. Ultimately, Rosa fought to keep her spirits high, and she returned ready to tackle leading the NAACP youth groups. Her goal was to inspire participants who would be the first generation to begin attending schools with white students.

Emmett Till and his Influence on Rosa Parks

Shortly after returning from the Highlander Workshop, Rosa Parks needed to use her renewed strength to continue fighting and inspiring youth. Within weeks of returning, the news of Emmett Till's murder had spread. This murder was jarring and memorable for many black Americans, particularly because Emmett's mother refused to be silent about the injustice. Emmett was living in the north but was kidnapped and murdered by a white man while visiting his grandfather in Mississippi. The attack took place, because Emmett was accused of flirting with a white woman. The death was gruesome. The amount of damage inflicted on Emmett's body still lingers in the writing of many contemporary black Americans. Till's mother refused to let her son's body stay in Mississippi and demanded it be returned to Chicago where she lived. Though this transport was almost prevented by the local police force, Till's mother won and was allowed to bring her son's body back to Illinois. Upon discovering the damage done to the body she held a service with an open casket and allowed a publication to share images of Emmett Till. The casket was seen by over 50,000 people. The horrors done to Emmitt Till broke Rosa Parks in a new way, and she refused to be silenced any longer. This would all take place just before the Bus Boycott started by Rosa's refusal to give up her seat.

The Bus, The Boycott, and All That Followed

Rosa Parks' History with Buses

Rosa Parks spoke often about her negative experiences with bus travel. Around the time of Emmett Till's death and for a long time prior, bus travel was a negative but essential method of transportation for most black Americans. Black travelers paid the same fare and used the bus with greater frequency than white Americans, yet they were often treated terribly. Because the mistreatment took place in front of white passengers, they felt entitled to also treat black passengers terribly. While there were many cities which continued the practice of segregation on busses in 1955, Montgomery tried to discontinue this practice. Despite no longer having signs that stated where black people were allowed to sit, it was still commonly enforced through intimidation by white people. In addition, bus drivers were legally allowed to force black riders to move, either out of preference or to give up their seats to white passengers. It wasn't only the seating arrangement that made the rides difficult; many drivers refused to let black people walk past white passengers. There were some drivers who would berate the black passengers and force them to exit the bus, then pay again to reenter the bus through the back. Some drivers ignored black people waiting for the bus. If the drivers did let black passengers onto the bus, they would often demean them verbally, shouting obscenities. Rosa was disheartened by these experiences, and she also spoke often about how difficult it was to watch these experiences take place in front of children. She was saddened by the thought that children were being taught to devalue themselves as people from a very young age.

These experiences were heightened within the state of Alabama. What few people know about bus segregation in Alabama, specifically Montgomery, is that in the early 1900s when segregation began black residents of Montgomery boycotted and won a change to the city ordinance specifying that no one was required to give up their seat if no other seat was available. What the city ordinance stated versus what was practiced in the community was a completely different story. Between 1945 and 1955 there were numerous cases in which black service members, who felt nearly equal while serving in the military, returned only to receive worse treatment in the

States. In 1944 Viola White, an employee of Maxwell Air Force Base, was physically abused and arrested for refusing to give her seat to a white passenger. When she took the case to court, it was postponed continuously, because the city knew it would not win the case. Police officers retaliated against Ms. White, raping her daughter as a form of punishment for attempting to take the city to court. A year later Geneva Johnson was arrested for "having an attitude" and incorrect payment. Four years later, Hilliard Brooker, a veteran, was arrested for refusing to reenter through the back door. Evidently, regardless of what the ordinance actually stated, white citizens refused to give up the idea of segregation in Montgomery for quite some time, and black Americans continued to be mistreated by the legal system.

Raymond and Rosa both hated the way bus drivers treated black passengers, and they often did their best to avoid riding the bus if possible. Many black community members of Montgomery were beginning to take smaller stands in response to their mistreatment of black passengers. The first major case of resistance was not Rosa Parks' stand, however, but that of Claudette Colvin. It was March 2, 1955 when Claudette, then 15 years old, left high school and boarded the bus home. That day Claudette and many of her classmates studied the US Constitution and realized how often their constitutional rights were challenged. When the bus driver demanded the black students move so that white passengers could sit, Colvin refused, even though some of her classmates had moved. A white woman refused to sit across from Colvin. The transit police were called, and they met her at the next stop. Claudette was then arrested. The police taunted Claudette, referring to her as a "thing" and making remarks about her body. Although she was only 15 at the time, many Montgomery citizens praised her strength. Her bail was paid by her parents. The night of her release her parents and neighbors kept guard, knowing people had been lynched for far less. This was one of the incidents that helped Rosa Parks find her own strength soon after and one that paved the way for change.

Taking a Stand By Refusing to Stand

Less than a year later, the air was tense with the possibility of drastic change. Rosa Parks was consistently working with the youth of the NAACP, training them to challenge segregation and how to act with the police should they be arrested. On the evening of December 1, 1955 Rosa was exhausted, since she worked a long day, as she usually did. She was thrilled at the prospect of relaxing at home that evening even if she had more work to do for the NAACP. Partly due to her usual workweek exhaustion, Parks didn't notice who the bus driver was. In numerous interviews she claimed that had she realized who the driver was, she wouldn't have gotten on the bus, because he had given her trouble before. Parks was with some of her workmates that evening. What some people don't know is that prior to this evening, Parks hadn't been asked directly to move for a white passenger. Sometime in the middle of her ride home, the white section filled up, and a passenger stood by the bus driver. The bus driver asked Rosa and her workmates to move from their seats. This was legal in the state of Alabama, but in Montgomery people weren't supposed to be asked to give up their seat if no other seat was available. It was in that moment Rosa realized she would not move. She made her decision and stuck to it regardless of what happened around her. While some people think it was her exhaustion that made her refuse to move, that was not the reason. Rather, Rosa thought about Emmett Till and Claudette. She also thought that moving meant she agreed with what was being done. While Rosa's colleagues did choose to move, Rosa refused, knowing full well that she was at risk of being sexually assaulted, arrested, or killed. The bus driver threatened Rosa and reminded her he had every right to have her arrested. Rosa knew this, and still she refused to move. At the next stop the police were waiting for Rosa to arrest her. They checked with the bus driver to see if he wanted to continue pressing charges. Rosa realized he could have just had her evicted but instead chose to press charges. It was this choice, his willingness and desire to see Parks punished, that led to a monumental change in history.

The Arrest

Rosa Parks was taken to city hall and found this arrest very much an irritant. Rosa previously commented that she had plenty of work to do for the NAACP and found the arrest to be distracting and a waste of her time. For some time after being arrested, the police refused to let Rosa use the telephone. They didn't allow her to drink water for some time either. Raymond later commented that he was furious it took so long for him to find out about her arrest. A fellow passenger lived near the Parks and could easily have told Raymond about the arrest. He chose not to, which caused Rosa to remain in jail longer. While in the cell, Rosa learned her cellmate had been in there for two months with no opportunity to contact her family. When Rosa was released, she made it a point to contact the woman's family and let them know where she was. Thankfully, the Durrs, a white family friend, and E.D. Nixon brought bail money and had Rosa released. They found her very calm and peaceful if not a little bothered.

After the arrest E.D. Nixon and the Durrs persuaded Rosa to team up with the NAACP and to use this arrest as a start to protest the bus segregation on a large scale. At first Rosa's family didn't think it a good idea, given the organization's lack of support for the young Claudette after her arrest. If they decided to pursue this as a case rather than simply working to get the charges dropped, it would be a long and difficult journey but one that the NAACP, E.D. Nixon, and the Durrs believed would bring about lasting change. Rosa knew this was a time when change could truly happen. They had worked hard staging small protests, and a case like this was needed to bring statewide and national attention to bus segregation. Thus, after some pondering, Rosa decided she would follow through regardless of the energy it would cost her.

The Boycott

The evening after the arrest was filled with tension and a sense of waiting by everyone around Rosa. It was the Women's Political Council (WPC) that decided to take the next step without consulting Rosa. Rosa was scheduled to appear in court Monday after her arrest to discuss the charges. The WPC decided to schedule a boycott of the Montgomery bus system that same day. Jo Ann Robinson spent the evening of Rosa's arrest printing thousands of leaflets that demanded all black people avoid the bus on Monday to prove they would no longer stand for the being treated unfairly. In only three hours the following morning, a team of men and women distributed over 35,000 pamphlets. Once they heard about the boycott, most people agreed to avoid the bus and were willing to walk however far was needed that Monday. In the days that followed, people around the city met in an effort to find ways to show their support of Rosa Parks. E.D. Nixon spoke with Martin Luther King, Jr., who was also in support of the protest. In addition, he met with white reporter Jo Azbell to give him full coverage of the coming boycott. Jo Azbell printed the leaflet in its entirety on the front page the Sunday before the boycott. Anyone who had not seen a flier would come to know about the boycott from the newspaper.

The morning of the court hearing came quickly, and many waited in anticipation to see who would show their support of the boycott. Robinson found herself enthusiastic and hopeful as she watched bus after bus go by with no black passengers on board. Rosa prepared for her court hearing and arrived early. She was greeted by hundreds of people outside who demonstrated their support of her. Inside the courtroom seats were filled to capacity. Those who could not find a seat stood in the hallway. Reporter Azbell wrote about a pervasive feeling of tension, which was fueled by blacks separated from whites in the gallery. The court case went about as well as could be expected, given recent history. The charges changed from a city focus to a state focus. The bus driver admitted that no other seats were available, while white passengers who testified claimed there were open seats. Ultimately Rosa was fined, but she and her legal team decided to appeal the case. Many showed their support for Rosa Parks in the coming days, and the boycott lasted much longer than originally anticipated.

About a week after the initial boycott, activists organized a carpool type system, because many people decided to stop riding the bus altogether. People were walking regardless of weather and collaborating in an effort to figure out new methods of transportation. This was one of the first times in history when blacks, regardless of political and religious views, banded together on a large scale to provide services to each other that weren't being provided by their community in support of Rosa Parks' protest. At Christmas the protest was still in effect, and Parks began reaching out to colleagues of her Highlander Retreat hopeful they would show their support in whatever ways possible. Upon hearing about the boycott from Rosa, many replied that they were astonished she was the one leading it. They originally viewed her as a quiet individual, but no one realized her strength or innate sense of when and where to be bold. They ultimately began showing their support and sent help however they could, whether in the form of footwear or money. The boycott continued for some time, and news of it spread beyond the city. People were furious at the attention the event was gathering, and the Parks received regular death threats, as did the King and Nixon families. The boycott itself started having a much more drastic effect on each of the participants. Both of the Parks eventually lost their jobs as a result of being affiliated with the boycott. While the bus company initially did not want to admit how much the boycott affected them, it was easily proved based on how angry people were. The boycott continued for over a year, and it was a time when Rosa felt the most support she had ever felt from her community.

Rosa's Later Activism

In the Years That Followed the Boycott

A few months after the boycott began, both Raymond and Rosa lost their jobs. That same year Raymond suffered a nervous breakdown and began seeing a psychiatrist. Attention being paid to the boycott meant that Rosa's time was being consumed by interviews, speeches, and travel—much of which was now being done on foot—yet there was little support for the family financially. Most of these events were unpaid. During the year of 1956 Rosa traveled often. This took a toll on her family members, who were often on the receiving end of the threats aimed at Rosa herself. Many involved with the boycott were said to sleep holding guns due to fear of retaliation from pro-segregationist whites. Pressure continued to build, which led to Raymond drinking heavily. Rosa continued raising awareness, even traveling as far as Washington DC and San Francisco to speak at national conferences. It wasn't until November 13, 1956 after an appeal that the Supreme Court deemed segregation unconstitutional both at a national and state level. This decision was a major win for all involved. In Montgomery on December 20, for the first time black citizens boarded the bus and sat wherever they pleased. People were shocked. Many thanked Rosa Parks for this change. Shortly afterward, *Look* magazine staged a photo shoot in which the reporter, a white man, sat behind Mrs. Rosa Parks, who sat in the front of the bus. The picture became one of the most memorable to date. What few people know is that the photo was taken on a bus being driven by James Blake, the man who called to have Rosa Parks arrested that infamous day over a year prior.

After the Supreme Court decision the NAACP turned their attention to a new focus: raising voter registration in the black community. This new focus, along with the decision to desegregate, was not all that helpful to the Parks family, however. Few establishments wanted to hire them, and both Rosa and Raymond struggled to find long-term work. Rosa continued traveling, even returning to speak at Highlander with students who were struggling with school desegregation and needing encouragement. During this post-boycott time, the Montgomery Improvement Association (MIA) and Martin Luther King, Jr. began employing people, including a personal secretary to King. The MIA, however, did not offer a permanent position to the Parks family, and it's not known exactly why.

From time to time they did raise funds to help offset expenses she incurred due to participation in the boycott.

Exclusion and Being Forced to Move

Staying in Montgomery proved to be detrimental to the health of Rosa, Raymond, and Leona. Rosa began having mild heart attacks. The MIA refused to give either of the Parks a permanent job and would not disclose why. Though Rosa was offered a contract to write a book about the boycott, she had no time to devote to the project. While the Highlander school eventually wound up paying her on a monthly basis, it took many free speeches and much work on Rosa's part to get to a point where they made the effort to compensate her. After realizing that Rosa would not cut back her work with the NAACP in Montgomery, Leona convinced her daughter and son-in-law to move with her to Detroit where they could be closer to Rosa's younger brother, Sylvester. Rosa agreed, as she continued to struggle financially and dealt with backlash from her own community and those involved in the civil rights movement. Many were bothered by the national attention she was receiving. People thought she gave speeches for attention, and they attempted to negate much of the work she did off stage. This was not surprising given that many people during this time were economically blacklisted. In addition to difficulty finding employment, many were being ignored by their own community due to fear of facing backlash themselves.

Shortly after moving to Detroit, Rosa was offered a position at the Hampton Institute in Virginia. The position offered her a steady salary, but because of the location, she had to live on campus away from her family. During this time she suffered from a severe ulcer, which left her unable to eat solid food, causing her to lose a lot of weight. Back at home Raymond and Leona were frequently ill, and so were other members of the family. The poverty was taxing physically and emotionally. The family continued struggling financially. Sylvester's family had little food, while Raymond contracted pneumonia and was hospitalized while Rosa was away. Rosa was enthusiastic with the students at the college. She was inspired by them and they, in turn, by her. Though she only stayed for one semester, she was able to save a little bit of money to bring home that holiday season. Once home Rosa knew there was no way she could return to the college. Raymond continued to be unemployed, and after the holidays Rosa tried to get a job as a seamstress. The family still struggled financially. While Rosa continued speaking and raising money for various organizations, few people cared enough to provide her with a stable income. Papers ran articles listing her struggles. The Parks failed to keep many apartments for long and were evicted with great frequency. During this time it was exceedingly difficult for black women to find work in the north after moving from the south, even more than black men. While the NAACP had begun hiring more and more women and men for salaried positions, they were setting a requirement for college degrees which Rosa Parks did not have. The stress took a toll on Parks, causing her to eventually need surgery for ulcers and a tumor on her throat. Her lack of insurance meant these costs would be paid out of pocket. When she was unable to afford the payments, the bill went to collections, and the family sank deeper into debt.

Joining Politics

In November 1964, John Conyers became one of only two elected blacks in the House of Representatives in Detroit. Rosa Parks had been working for some time as a volunteer on the Conyers campaign. Her decision to support Conyers would eventually lead to her first steady employment in many years. After being elected as congressman in March of the following year, Conyers hired Rosa permanently as part of his administrative team. This position gave Rosa a steady salary, health insurance, and a chance to continue doing the activist work she had long been doing. John Conyers valued her history, connection to the community, and intelligence. He valued her experience in the civil rights movement and thought she was one of the most important activists alive. As part of her employment she frequently went with Conyers where he was needed, whether she served as a greeter for his meetings or as support alongside him at the podium. Her work continued for most of her life. While she enjoyed much of the work, her time in Detroit was not much different from her time in Montgomery. Rosa frequently commented on the racism that existed in the north. While many thought it a better place because of the lack of segregation, there were still ways segregation happened legally. The housing situation was terrible for most black Americans, the schools were overcrowded and underfunded, and job opportunities were scarce. Rosa knew many of these issues stemmed from racial inequality and were not just a matter of being in the north or south. There were clear divisions in the housing situation, the way adults treated each other, and the way youth were treated, as well. With the help of Conyers, Rosa and many other black Americans were hopeful for change in Detroit and beyond.

When the Parks family moved to Detroit, there was a mass influx of black residents. The population nearly doubled, and by the '60s most black Americans had moved farther north. During this same time the suburbs grew in population, and many of the city dwelling white people moved to these suburbs. After this took place much of the city of Detroit began to be labeled as risky and unfit for investment. There were efforts in Detroit to keep black people trapped by raising the rent because of overpopulation. This was another form of segregation that was taking place. While homes were readily available for purchase, developers were allowed to say whether or not they would sell to black families. Even with thousands of vacant homes available, few were actually available to the growing numbers of black families in need. In 1967 Detroit claimed to have the largest number of black homeowners in the country, but the focus should have been elsewhere. While black Americans owned many of these homes, the houses were at a standard far below that of their white neighbors. There were strong attempts to keep white people within their own communities and black people within theirs. Likewise, because the houses were in overpopulated areas, many black residents were paying much more than their white neighbors for much less. As the housing situation worsened and the population grew, so did the idea of ghettos and police brutality. By the mid-1960s the city of Detroit was having multiple instances of police brutality and police killings of low-income black residents. A general uneasiness grew between white and black residents of the same city. Conyers tried to warn city officials that tensions were rising, and very soon they would be dealing with a riot like many seen in the southern states. People were tired of being treated unfairly, much like conditions prior to the bus boycott. During the years 1964 through 1968 there were mass riots in nearly every major American city. People were refusing to sit back and be mistreated.

On July 23, 1967 police raided a bar that was open illegally after hours. These establishments were frequently used as meeting places for black activists and black workers who worked late hours. The owners kept the bars open late to allow for extra income as well as offer a community space. Conyers attempted to calm the crowd and help disperse it, but instead people began fighting back. By the next evening thousands of black Americans had gathered, and the riot extended over 14 square miles. The police were shocked at the size of the crowd, and they pushed back against everyone involved, not just those who seemed to be involved in illegal activities. The police attacked buildings and private homes on the basis that rioters were in hiding. In addition, many black owned businesses, meeting places for black activists, were severely damaged. The riots gave police an opportunity to do what they wanted to do regardless of how brutal the treatment was. Within a matter of days as many as 10,000 people were arrested for their involvement in the riot. The jails overflowed, and makeshift cells had to be formed out of empty busses. Thirty people were killed by police, and 13 others were killed as a result of moving through the riot. Much of Detroit was unable to recover after this event. City structures were permanently damaged. Businesses were unable to reopen. During the riot Raymond and Rosa watched from their apartment as fires broke out, looting occurred, and equipment was stolen from Raymond's barber shop. The two were afraid of what would come of the events, but they understood the suffering that drove people to their breaking points.

After the riot in Detroit, the city struggled to rebuild, and so did the Parks family. There was a revolution taking place. With the Black Power Movement growing, black Americans attempted to reclaim their African heritage. Rosa, even with her many health concerns, did her best to be present at any event nearby that was related to black pride, but especially anything related to supporting black youth. In the early 1970s Rosa helped launch the Joanne Little Defense League, which aimed to support justice for women who faced sexual violence and arrests which resulted from such acts. Because of the awareness Rosa had already raised around these problems, the Black Panther Movement began to take gender issues more seriously and considered them as important as issues of race. Parks continued to advocate for people who were being arrested, and she aimed to raise awareness of the modern criminal system and how it treated its prisoners.

Rosa Parks' Health and Raymond's Death

The late 1970s were a difficult time for Rosa Parks. She still traveled and spoke with great frequency, and never relinquished her part in the civil rights movement. But the health of her mother and husband were suffering. One of Rosa's nieces moved in to help her care for the two while Rosa was away on speaking engagements. Rosa's ulcers continued to worsen despite the surgery she underwent. Even though Rosa had a better income, the family as a whole was struggling financially. All around the same time Raymond, Leona, and Sylvester developed cancer. Sylvester and his wife had 13 children, some of whom were still in early childhood. After battling throat cancer for five years, Raymond Parks died in 1977. Only three months after Raymond's death she lost her brother Sylvester to cancer, as well. Rosa was heartbroken, but she didn't have the opportunity to grieve either death. Two years after the death of Sylvester, her mother passed away, as well. It seemed Rosa's life was flipped upside down in a matter of years, and there was little she could do. With no other income but her own, Rosa struggled. People attempted to raise donations, but such efforts failed to produce enough income, especially given that Rosa was now nearing her seventies. People thought kindly of Rosa and repeatedly asked her to speak and inspire, but few were willing to help make her life easier.

After the deaths of her loved ones, Rosa didn't know what to do except continue her political involvement. She advocated for Jesse Jackson during his race for the presidential Democrat nomination. She met and conversed with Nelson Mandela. She marched. She protested. She educated. She never slowed down because of her age or many losses in life.

The Later Years of Rosa Parks' Life, Her Death, and Her Legacy

Struggling In Her Later Years

In 1994 when Rosa Parks was 84 years old, she was mugged by a local resident of Detroit. Joseph Skipper, a young black man, pretended to ward off an assailant, asked for a tip, and then followed Rosa to her bedroom. He stole the remainder of Rosa's money after punching her in the face repeatedly. The media used this as an opportunity to say that younger individuals were losing their morals, but Rosa was very forgiving of the situation. She portrayed it as an issue of the black community not being supported enough. In addition, many people apprehended and punished Skipper for harming Rosa. In the 5 to 10 years prior to this assault, Rosa was growing tired of the frequent interviews and articles that focused on her stance during the bus incident. While she visited Montgomery on the 20-year anniversary of this event, she still tired of reliving the memory. It was a painful one for her, but one she repeatedly stated she would do again and again, even knowing all the harm it brought into her personal life. In an *Ebony* article, it was noted that Parks felt people focused only on this one moment in a larger movement. She wanted people to recognize all the work that came before and followed it. Still, she continued to fly across the country and gave many more speeches. By doing so she continually brought attention to efforts needed to create change.

Parks worked tirelessly in her later years. She was at the forefront of recognizing Martin Luther King, Jr. Day as a national holiday. She worked to raise awareness of black history and attempted to insure that her colleagues in the movement were not too whitewashed after their deaths. She wanted people to understand the movement and the actionable steps it took to succeed in bringing about more equality. Often people seemed to link the movement to big grand gestures but did not recognize the tireless small daily efforts required to achieve goals. Thankfully, much of her work was being recognized nationally, and she finally started to receive more national attention. In 1991 the Smithsonian placed a bust of her image in the museum, but her greatest honor would arrive in 1999. After hundreds of letters and telephone calls from supporters of Parks were received, Rosa was granted the Congressional Gold Medal. Though there was much happiness about this honor being granted, many pointed out the irony of the government's willingness to honor individuals only years later when they had become too weak to engage in much more activism. Rosa, however, was grateful for the recognition even if it came very late in her life. The following year a museum was built in Rosa Parks' honor at the same location where she had refused to stand. This was a shock to Rosa who repeatedly stated that she had no idea one day could lead to so much more.

The Death of Rosa Parks

On October 24, 2005 Rosa Parks passed away in her Detroit home. Her death was a national tragedy and one that was used by the government to bring back hope in the black community after their failure to provide for the victims of Hurricane Katrina. John Conyers, Jr. employed Parks during her last 20 years. He proposed that she be honored by having her casket displayed in the Capitol Rotunda, an honor only previously granted to one other African American, a man. People mailed letters, made telephone calls, and visited in-person to demand she be honored in this way until Congress agreed. Her funeral service proved to be exceptionally well-attended. Before arriving in Washington DC, her casket was placed in Montgomery, where a two-day service was held in her honor. She was then transported to the Metropolitan African Methodist Episcopal Church for another public service which allowed more people to pay their respects. Following this she was sent to Detroit for a viewing at the Museum of African American History. She finally arrived at Detroit's Greater Grace Temple on November 2 for a seven-hour funeral service. It seemed even in death Rosa still traveled far to share her many causes. After the funeral President Bush ordered a statue be built in her honor and placed in the US Capitol as a symbol of respect and admiration for her actions. Rosa Parks was the first African American to have a statue placed in the Capitol. In the three days following her death, all of the Montgomery city busses placed ribbons in the front seats to honor her legacy and show people the importance of the civil rights movement.

The Legacy of Rosa Parks

Today most schools across the nation teach the history of Rosa Parks and her refusal to stand, but Rosa left behind a legacy larger than that of her bus protest. In 1987 she and others cofounded the Rosa and Raymond Parks Institute for Self Development. The program aimed to show youth their full potential, and this was done partly through the development of programs that created cross-cultural awareness. In 1980, in association with the foundation, the *Detroit News* and Detroit Public Schools began a Rosa Parks scholarship opportunity that currently awards about 40 scholarships in the amount of $2,000 each to high school seniors who show qualities like those of Parks. The institute's main purpose aside from the scholarship is to run the "Pathways to Freedom" tour. On this tour youth are taken to important stops along the underground railroad which show the importance of the civil rights movement. In addition to the institute and the scholarship, Troy University has an official Rosa Parks museum where visitors can learn about the bus boycott, Rosa Parks' life, and see modern exhibits that focus on black history. This museum attempts to connect Rosa's past with modern movements being led by contemporary black activists and artists.

On the 60th anniversary of the bus boycott, Barack Obama spoke about Rosa Parks' history and the influence it had on his becoming the first African American president. Her legacy continues to resonate with people. Countless television series, books, and monuments have been created to mark her importance in history. During her life Rosa was awarded numerous recognitions including the Martin Luther King, Jr. award from the NAACP, a Presidential Medal of Freedom, and the Governor's Medal of Honor for Extraordinary Courage. She was also named one of the country's 20 most influential people by *Time* magazine. When Nelson Mandela visited the US after his release, Rosa was part of the welcoming group. In 1992 Rosa finally published her autobiography which recounted the vast contributions she made throughout her life.

The Importance of Learning the Real History of Rosa Parks

Rosa Parks is a respected and well-known individual, but how much does the general public actually know about her beyond her actions aboard the bus that fateful day? It is important to study her history because of its deep connection to the struggles of black Americans and because of her role in the civil rights movement. Very few people know the many ways Rosa showed the value of grassroots organizing. Rosa Parks was not as quiet and gentle as she was often portrayed. She was a woman who was constantly working behind the scenes to raise awareness about important issues faced by black Americans. She fought to support prominent black leaders and worked tirelessly to show her support for black youth. In the years that followed the deaths of her family members, Rosa rarely slowed in her work, only stepping away when her health or home life demanded it. She continued supporting potential presidential candidates, reforms, national holidays for black leaders, and more. In fact, Rosa was part of the reason people celebrate Martin Luther King, Jr. Day.

It is important that Rosa's history and her struggles not be forgotten. While she was remembered for her actions on the bus, few knew that she struggled as a result of income inequality, racial tensions, and health issues that frequently plague black, low income Americans. Despite her constant touring and speaking engagements, Rosa made very little income and was unable to fully support herself at many points in her life. Only a few years before her death, Parks was at risk of being evicted from the apartment she had lived in since 1994 because of her inability to pay rent. Thankfully, after much prodding, the apartment management company agreed to let Rosa stay in her apartment rent free for the remainder of her life. This alone shows the necessity of taking care of our activists and leaders early in life and not just after death.

Printed in Great Britain
by Amazon